WALK THE

TWENTY WALKS AROUND AND ABOVE GREAT LANGDALE, LITTLE LANGDALE, CHAPEL STILE, ELTERWATER AND SKELWITH BRIDGE

BY

B³.11

BILL BIRKETT

B.²2eH

BILL BIRKETT PUBLISHING

PUBLISHED BY BILL BIRKETT PUBLISHING

This book is dedicated to the memory of Jackson Corrie whose love of The Langdales and freedom of the hills was a philosophy for life; Jackson never passed a hitchhiker by, he took scores of children through The Cathedral clutching candles, he opened his home and gave his time freely to all and anyone simply prepared to give the Langdale experience a try.

Cover photograph: Over Elter Water to the Langdale Pikes
Backcover photographs: Neddy Boggle Stone Elterwater Common - Walk 3, Blea Tarn with Langdale Pikes behind - Walk 14, The maple tree in the centre of Elterwater Village - Walks 4 & 5, Cathedral Quarry in Little Langdale - Walk 18, Slaters Bridge Little Langdale Walk 18.
Page 1 photograph: A view over Chapel Stile up Great Langdale

All photographs from the Bill Birkett Photo Library
Maps by Martin Bagness based on pre-1950 Ordnance Survey maps. Completely redrawn 2009

First published in the UK in 2009
Reprinted in 2011, 2012, 2013, 2014 (Twice), 2015 (Twice) & 2016.

Copyright © Bill Birkett 2009

A catalogue record for this book is available from The British Library

ISBN 978-0-9564296-0-5

Book Design by Bill Birkett
Printed in Bowness by Badger Press
for Bill Birkett Publishing
www.billbirkett.co.uk

DISCLAIMER
Walking in the country and over the fells is potentially dangerous activity and each individual following the routes described within this book is responsible for their own safety and actions. Neither the author nor the publisher accepts any responsibility for the individual safety or actions of anyone using this book. Although the author encountered no difficulty of access on the routes described, and while considerable effort has been made to avoid so doing, the inclusion of a route does not imply that a right of way or right of access exists in every case or in all circumstances. Readers are also advised that changes can occur to the landscape that may affect the contents of this book. The author welcomes notification of any such changes.

[iii]

CONTENTS

The Langdales

The Walks Map

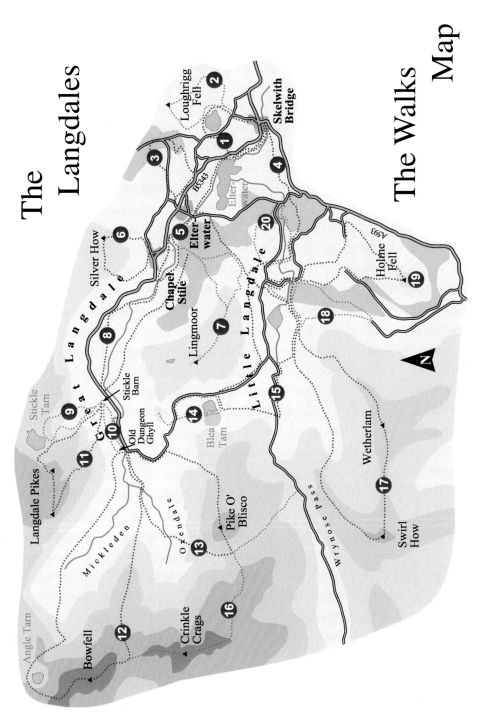

INTRODUCTION – WALK THE LANGDALES

Great Langdale is one of the most popular mountain valleys in the whole of Britain. Oxendale and Mickleden, at the head of the valley, display a rugged and spectacular skyline of high fells; The Langdale Pikes, Bowfell, Crinkle Crags and Pike O'Blisco. These fine ridges, airy tops and rocky steeps have long been a favourite with hill walkers, mountaineers and rock climbers. Yet, as important as the high fells are, and they have been my great passion for over fifty years, they are only a part of The Langdales' experience.

The name Great Langdale comes directly from the Viking; 'Gurt Langel', in the local parlance, which simply means 'great long valley'. This long 'S' shaped valley wriggles it's way for some 12km through much varied scenery. Its dramatic start beneath the high mountains wanders on through farm meadows to the villages of Chapel Stile and Elterwater. It continues by the woods of to Elter Water lake and over Skelwith Force waterfall to its effective terminus at Skelwith Bridge beneath the end of Loughrigg Fell.

Yet that is only part of the story, for there are two very beautiful Langdale Valleys; Great and Little. Each has its own intrinsic character, each a wealth of interest. The valleys are separated by Lingmoor Fell, their rivers merge in Elter Water to flow on, as the River Brathay, to finally pass beneath the Skelwith Bridge.

The heads of both the valleys are surrounded by high fells, hanging basins and mountain tarns. Wetherlam, Swirl How and Carrs which fall to Wrynose Pass and the Three Shires Stone surround the head of Little Langdale. Great Langdale is enclosed bythehighest of the fells including the iconic Langdale Pikes. Between the two, the wild and remote Blea Tarn basin. These classic glacially formed U shaped valleys offer a myriad of interest within the nooks and folds, wild woods, tumbling waterfalls, lake and meadow. A landscape of much diversity, hosting a rich association of wildlife.

Man's involvement with this fascinating world has spanned for over seven thousand years and adds yet another dimension of interest. Throughout this long history The Langdales have meant many things to many different peoples. Alongside the mines and quarries, the pastures and meadow, the stone cottages, farms and packhorse bridges, there are the remnants of many long forgotten industries. These range from the Neolithic Stone Axe Factory, high amongst The Langdale Pikes, to the great mill wheels of the 20th C Gunpowder Works scattered around The Langdale Estate. The hill farmers in both these mountain valleys still breed the hardy Herdwick sheep first introduced by The Vikings.

Based on local knowledge accrued over my lifetime this practical walking guidebook offers a mixture of routes of varying length and difficulty; both high and low level fells, river walks, waterfalls, woods and quarries, and following ancient byways and paths by farm, cottage and over stone arch bridge. The walks are all circular, all my favourites and, whatever the season or prevailing weather (within reason of course – be sensible) there is a good spread of choice here for most people. These routes are always changing, with every season, with each nuance of light. Furthermore there are many excellent inns, cafes and places to rest all of which are detailed in this book. I personally recommend the superb locally brewed ales.

Whilst I have written, and photographically illustrated a number of books on the subject of walking, climbing and the great outdoors, including my prize winning photographic essay 'A Year In The Life of the Langdale Valleys', (published by Frances Lincoln) and 'Complete Lakeland Fells', regarded as the single most definitive book on the Lakeland Fells, it may seem surprising to many that I have waited so long to produce this book. Well, despite the fact I was born and bred in The Langdales and love the area beyond compare, until now I have always felt there was a wider picture to paint. Indeed, in this respect, I am still busily engaged on a number of projects.

So be it, but I felt the time was now right for this practical guidebook. It is the first book published by **Bill Birkett Publishing** (copies available direct – see my website *billbirkett.co.uk* for contact details) and similar books in the series are planned and in production. For me to walk and photograph these marvellous routes, with friends, family and our Collie, 'Jet', and to meet with many kindred spirits doing likewise, has been an absolute joy.

Above all else, I hope it's the same for you.

WALK 1

SKELWITH BRIDGE TO LOUGHRIGG TARN

A heady mix of river, waterfall, a lake, two tarns, mixed woods and fine vistas make this
a delightful and enchanting outing. From Skelwith Bridge proceed up the River Brathay
to pass Skelwith Force waterfall, the Brathay Meadows, Elter Water and Rob Rash Wood.
Above the woods find Loughrigg Tarn and the superlative viewpoint of Crag Head
before descent leads to the circuit of Loughrigg Tarn. The little road below Tarn Foot leads
down directly to Skelwith Bridge.

THE ROUTE

Go through the village or head towards Langdale until possible to skirt left through the open stoneworks yard where local Lakeland Slate and attractive stone is polished and cut (proceed up the road a little further when work in progress) to gain the path by the river. In 150m Skelwith Force and viewpoint can be found down to the left. Continue along the path through the meadows by the River Brathay to the foot of Elter Water lake. Enter Rob Rash Wood to find in 100m a track ascending diagonally right up the wood. Cross the road to a kissing gate and up again through the wood following the path which bears right to a little ladder stile over a stone wall. Go left, boggy, and follow a narrow path towards a notch in the shoulder. To the left, just before reaching the high point, lies Little Loughrigg Tarn – now heavily choked with reeds.

In front lies a fine view to Loughrigg Tarn and directly below a stone cottage. Descend the path for only a few metres to find a narrow path leading right up through the bracken to the rocky knolls top of Crag Head – Little Loughrigg. Superb views. Retrace your steps (or take one of the various other paths) to make descent towards the stone cottage to intercept a well defined path traversing down to the lane. Go left to pass the buildings of Loughrigg Fold and gain the road. Go left to find,

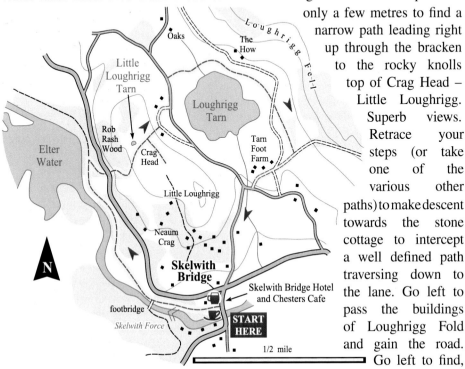

Over Loughrigg Tarn to The Langdale Pikes

on the right, a gate and stile leading down the field to a ladder stile over a wall from where the path skirts the edge of the tarn. The path moves left away

Skelwith Force waterfall

from the tarn and rises to a lane. Cross the lane and follow the little path up the field and on past the beechwood to intercept a stony track. Go right and follow the walled track to a gate. Keep straight on to pass the buildings around Tarn Foot then descend to the road. Go right then left down a lesser road (with parking by the junction) directly to Skelwith Bridge.

LENGTH: 4½km
TIME: 2 hours
DIFFICULTY: Easy though making a little ascent (200m) and descent
START & FINISH: Limited Parking beside the Langdale Road at Skelwith Bridge (344035)
ALTERNATIVE START: Limited parking at the head of the little road below Tarn Foot
MAPS: OS L90 or OL7
HOSTELRIES: Chesters Café and Skelwith Bridge Hotel

WALK 2

SKELWITH'S TARN FOOT TO LOUGHRIGG FELL

Offering expansive views from its summit, Loughrigg is a delightful and friendly fell with many fascinating nooks and crannies. This route, beginning from Tarn Foot, climbs by lane and track to Black Mire before ascending the heights and traversing to the summit trig point. Steep, straightforward descent leads to a traverse above Oaks and by The How to finally pass above Loughrigg Tarn.

THE ROUTE

Initially take the road heading towards Ambleside to find (in 25m) a lane to the left rising to Tarn Foot Farm and cottages. Continue to pass the cottages then go straight across the junction, gate, to find a lane. Climb the lane to emerge above the fell wall. Traverse above the wall, higher viewpoint, finally leaving it where the track begins to ascend to the moss of Black Mire. Climb until a good little path bears off to the left. The path soon intercepts a larger

FACT SHEET
LENGTH: 5km
TIME: 2½ hours
DIFFICULTY: Mildly difficult with steepish ascent (300m) and descent
START & FINISH: Limited parking around the head of the little road below Tarn Foot (346040)
ALTERNATIVE START: Limited Parking beside the Langdale Road at Skelwith Bridge
MAPS: OS L90 or OL7
HOSTELRIES: Nearest are Chesters Café and The Skelwith Bridge Hotel

path, climbing from Black Mire, then makes steep ascent towards the highest point (of the heights above Ivy Crag). Bear left around the shoulder and down slightly to a little valley containing two distinct little tarns. Cross and climb the main path over the next shoulder (with a cairned knoll to the left). Fall slightly then ascend into a narrowing corridor between the hummocks to climb steeply out to a level col. Dead ahead lies the summit trig point (to the left the tops known as the 'Three Sisters').

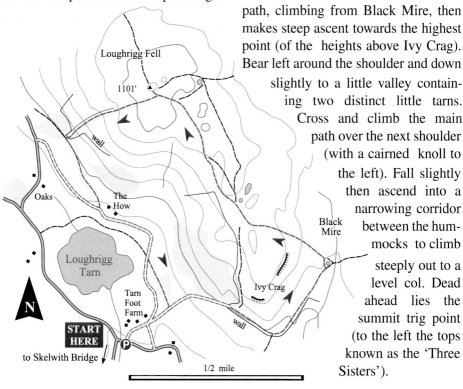

Above the fell wall with The Pikes beyond

Return to the col, cairn, and go right (south west), to make steep descent of the grass and then stone steps leading down the corridor formed by the little gill. At the bottom turn left and follow along above the fell wall until just before the buildings of The How a little gate leads right down to the main track. Turn left and follow the track, above Loughrigg Tarn, to a gate by the cottage. Go right to pass Tarn Foot and back to the road.

The 'Three Sisters' of Loughrigg Fell seen above The How and Loughrigg Tarn

ELTERWATER COMMON TO HUNTINGSTILE AND HIGH CLOSE

This walk consists of both extensive views and rich, fascinating woodland. Climbing to Huntingstile there are views over Elterwater Common to Wetherlam and The Langdale Pikes. From here a vista opens over Grasmere before descent by the top of Red Bank, above Deerbolt Woods, continues through the grounds of High Close and the connected Low Wood on National Trust Permitted Paths and trackways. An exploration of a largely forgotten magical world where the exotic Mediterranean Pine, Sequoia and ancient Lime mix with traditional woodland.

THE ROUTE

From the back of the car park walk over right, boggy, to find a better defined path ascending directly to the little brackened knoll above. A path leads to the road. Go right up the road until a well used path rises left up by the steam, past a little stone building, and up the depression to the level and boggy Huntingstile col. Bear right, stones across the bog, to follow right along the edge of the stone wall rising to a kissing gate and view over Grasmere. Descend the path traversing to the top of Red Bank. (Deerbolts Wood lays below). Go right along the road to the junction.

Just left of the nose of the junction is a little iron gate. Pass

through this into the wooded grounds of High Close now a Youth Hostel (National Trust Permitted Path). Some of the exotic trees have name plaques. Keep along the narrow path, straight on at junction, and descend to a broader path. Go right. Next junction go left (large house of High Close now behind rhododendrons to right) and

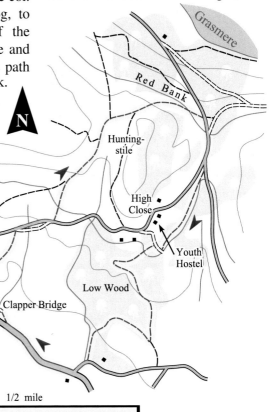

continue to descend with an open field and iron railings on the left. Don't go through either of the gates but go right to find another gate. Go left through this and follow the constructed track beneath Garden Cottages to wind down through the exquisite mixed woods of Low Wood. Keep on across the stream keeping to the main track until a field opens to the left.

Return to Elterwater Common with The Pikes beyond

Keep right at the bottom corner following along by the iron fence on the edge of the wood. Go right at the corner of the fence and decend down a little hill to a junction. Go left, cross two little wooden footbridges and, with open field to right, continue down the corridor to a little iron gate and stone stile onto the road to quit Low Wood. Go right then right again following the main road up Langdale to cross a cattle grid. Fine views open to the left, over Elterwater Common

Beech by the foot of Low Wood

to The Pikes. Descend a little then bear right, off the road, to follow an ancient track below the wall. Cross the little stone slab

clapper bridge and continue finally bearing left and gaining the path taken from the car park.

The kissing gate from Huntingstile which leads to the descent to the top of Red Bank, with the Vale of Grasmere seen beyond

FACT SHEET
LENGTH: 4km
TIME: 2 hours
DIFFICULTY: Easy, though making ascent (200m) and descent and a little boggy in places
START & FINISH: Car park on Elterwater Common (329051)
ALTERNATIVE START: Elterwater Village Car Park
MAPS: OS L90 or OL7
HOSTELRIES: Nearest are Eltermere Inn, Britannia Inn, Wainwrights' Inn and Brambles Café

WALK 4

A CIRCUIT OF ELTERWATER BENEATH THE LANGDALES

Starting from Elterwater this circuit contrasts open vista with wooded dale, traversing the foot of the Great and Little Langdale valleys. It rounds quiet Elter Water with classic views of the Langdale Pikes and visits two tumbling waterfalls.

THE ROUTE

Go left out of the car park and follow the road, over the bridge, towards Little Langdale. Continue to pass the Youth Hostel and then the entrance to Eltermere Hotel until a road branches up to the right. When the road becomes unsurfaced climb steeply (don't go right). Keep climbing the rough stony track, delightfully wooded it's known locally as Ullet's (Owl's) Nest and it climbs to cross over the brow of the hill into Little Langdale. In ascent pass through a gate and continue until the track levels. At this point a kissing gate on the left leads to a little path – signed Wilson Place Farm.

Follow the path and make descent leading to the farmyard Continue through the farm, descending to a junction with the main Little Langdale Road. Go left until in 90m a kissing

gate on the right leads down the meadow of Lang Parrock to a wooden footbridge crossing the River Brathay. The path continues to rise on the far side of the valley to gain a gate by the distinct white building of Stang End Farm.

Pass through the gates to a junction with the road and go left following the tarmac along to the next group of buildings, in 450m – High Park Farm. Go through the farmyard, bear right and then left to follow the track through the fields. A kissing gate leads into the woods. Go left following the little path which makes steep descent through the woods to the banks of the river. A little further downstream lies the waterfall of Colwith Force. Continue by the river until steps lead down beyond the fall. Go left to the rocky knoll viewpoint. Then back to follow along the path above the river to emerge from the woods over a stile onto the road. Bear right for 100m to a stile on the left. Cross the stile and the field

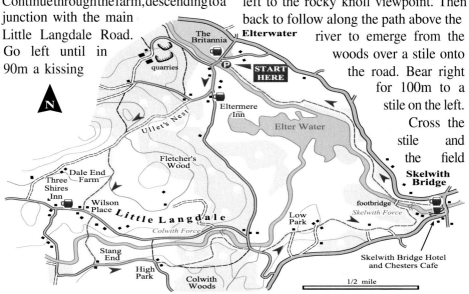

to make a steep climb through the wood to a higher field. Traverse the field, cross the lane and pass the buildings of Low Park. Continue to Park Farm. Take the track left through the farmyard and follow the signed Skelwith Bridge path. Bear right in the dip to pass the farmstead of Park House. Keep on the track until a path branches off to the left leading into the woods above Skelwith Bridge. After a little descent through the wood a path bears off left to a distinctive steel railing bridge crossing the river just above Skelwith Force waterfall. A short excursion to the right leads to the waterfall viewing point (a few hundred metres further down to the right lie the attractions of Skelwith Bridge; Chesters Café and Gallery, Skelwith Bridge Hotel.

Elterwater Village centre, the Maple Tree and Britannia Inn

Our route, however, goes left over the bridge to follow the wide trackway through the meadows alongside the river to the foot of Elter Water and a prize view to Langdale Pikes. Continue along the pathway into Rob's Rash Wood. Walk through the wood by the lake and on beside the river to return to the car park in Elterwater Village.

The Path by the foot of Elter Water

FACT SHEET
LENGTH: 8km
TIME: 3 hours
DIFFICULTY: Easy with short straightforward ascent and descent.
START & FINISH: Elterwater Village large car park (328048).
ALTERNATIVE STARTS: Little Langdale Village, Colwith Bridge, Skelwith Bridge, Silverthwaite Car Park.
MAPS: OS L90 or OL7.
HOSTELRIES: Britannia Inn and Eltermere Inn in Elterwater, Three Shires Inn in Little Langdale, Chesters Cafe and Skelwith Bridge Hotel at Skelwith Bridge

WALK 5

LANGDALE BECK WALK VIA ELTERWATER AND CHAPEL STILE

This easy circular walk crosses five bridges along the dashing Langdale Beck between Chapel Stile and Elterwater. It begins over Elterwater Bridge before proceeding along the true right bank of the river to Chapel Stile's New Bridge. Return is made through Thrang and Chapel Stile, to cross Chapel Stile Bridge below Wainwrights' Inn to complete the loop and follow back down the true right bank of the river to Elterwater. Pleasantly wooded by the river.

THE ROUTE

Cross Elterwater Bridge in the direction of Little Langdale. Immediately go right and follow the Elterwater Quarry road, lined by large blocks of slate, above the river. In some 300m, with a large barred ancient quarry tunnel to the left, the path drops off down to the right. Follow the path to Chapel Stile Bridge. Then go left following the path by the river to the right or left of the stone wall. Before the stone abutments and quarry bank, by a small building, bear right from the main path to follow the bank of the river. As the river bends go right across the small stone slab

Chapel Stile Bridge

bridge and continue up the river bank. Muddy when wet. Pass Tommy's Dub (pool) and continue to find a wooden footbridge crossing the channel carrying the stream known as Baysbrown Pool. Walk between the waters to find the stone arch of New Bridge. The inset plaque atop the bridge says it was built in 1818! Cross and continue along the stony track until at a junction go right up a walled lane to pass the buildings of Thrang. Beyond the buildings

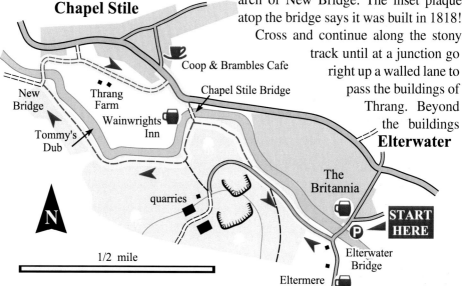

Chapel Stile

Coop & Brambles Cafe

Chapel Stile Bridge

New Bridge

Thrang Farm

Wainwrights Inn

Tommy's Dub

Elterwater

quarries

The Britannia

N

START HERE

P

1/2 mile

Elterwater Bridge

Eltermere Inn

Baysbrown Pool flowing to Langdale Beck

New Bridge

go right at the junction and follow the stony track beside the stone wall to descend to gain the road in the centre of Chapel Stile. Go right and pass Wainwrights' Inn to find a little gate on the right leading to Chapel Stile Bridge. Cross and go left to return by the original route.

FACT SHEET
LENGTH: 3½km
TIME: 1½ hours
DIFFICULTY: Easy, a little muddy by river, don't attempt when river flooded
START & FINISH: Elterwater village car park (328046)
ALTERNATIVE START: Car park on Elterwater Common, Chapel Stile village, Baysbrown Campsite
MAPS: OS L90 or OL7
HOSTELRIES: Britannia Inn, Eltermere Inn, Wainwrights' Inn, Brambles Cafe

CHAPEL STILE TO SILVER HOW BY MEGS GILL

A very fine route offering superlative views over both Great Langdale and the Vale of Grasmere. A path rises through the meadows of Chapel Stile to Walthwaite. Steeper ascent leads to an exposed traverse around the depths of Megs Gill and out onto the watershed between Langdale and Grasmere. Beyond lie Silver How and Youdell Tarn before zigzag descent beside Robin Gill gains a traverse to the rocky spire of Copt How. Finish via Thrang Quarry and under the church back into Chapel Stile.

THE ROUTE

On the opposite side of the road and 100m down from Wainwrights' Inn a signed footpath leads through a kissing gate and along beside a beech hedge. Continue through a little wood to emerge into the meadows and ascend to the Walthwaite road. Go left, pass the house named Walthwaite Lodge, to find a kissing gate above on the right. Zigzag up the fellside with the stone wall just to the right. At the top corner of the wall the path rises diagonally to traverse the true right bank of Megs Gill. The path is narrow and exposed though the going is straightforward. Continue to intercept a further path and go right climbing to a point beside the upper streambed of the gill. Cross the stream low on the right to find a rock path under the outcrop. The path continues across scree to make ascent to a flat grassy area on the shoulder.

Take the path climbing to the right side of the little crag and follow the high diagonal grassy path taking the easiest line through the undulations to the cairned top of Silver How. Outstanding views over the Vale of Grasmere and Rydal Water. Follow the grassy path heading west, boggy in places,

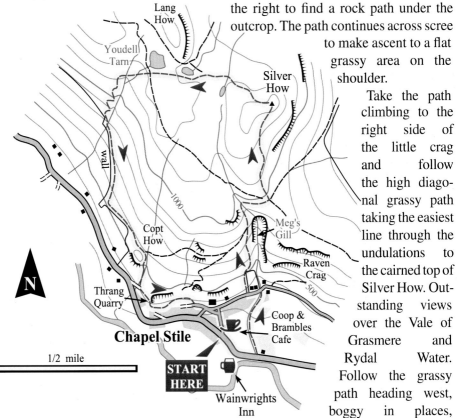

until beside a small unnamed tarn, with the distinct rocky nose of Lang How above and beyond, leave the main path and traverse left over a grassy shoulder. In the hollow lies a small tarn now virtually overgrown with reeds – Youdell Tarn. Descend by the outflowing stream and then traverse right

Looking to Copt How with The Langdale Pikes beyond.

crossing a further stream before the gill deepens. Follow down the true right bank of the ravine, Robin Gill, to find a series of zigzags leading down to a stone wall. Go left and follow along above the wall to find the gap leading up from Harry Place Farm. Traverse across the gap to find a further path following along above the next wall.

This path rises to a shoulder behind the rocky protuberance of Copt How. Behind there is a spectacular view to The Langdale Pikes. By the rock take the path bearing off down to the right to find some rock steps. A short scrambly section of rocky steps leads to a levelling from where the path leads off to the left. Pass over the slight rock outcrops following the well worn path down towards some boulders. Go left to intercept a grassy track just above the row of cottages. Ascend left to find the path leading down stone steps into the disused Thrang Quarry. Traverse through the quarry to find a lane leading down to a gate and entrance to the village with the church just beyond.

Over Youdell Tarn to the head of Great Langdale

FACT SHEET
LENGTH: 5¼km
TIME: 3 hours
DIFFICULTY: *Mildly difficult with strenuous ascent (some 400m) and descent. The path around Megs Gill is narrow and exposed in places.*
START & FINISH: *Chapel Stile, limited parking within the perimeter of the village (323052)*
ALTERNATIVE STARTS: *Elterwater Village, Elterwater Common and Baysbrown Campsite.*
MAPS: *OS L90 or OL7*
HOSTELRIES: *Wainwrights' Inn and Brambles Café in Chapel Stile*

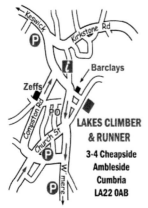

LINGMOOR FELL FROM CHAPEL STILE

An evocative name for the lovely heather-clad fell which separates the Langdales and gives spectacular views. Utilising a network of quarry-men's tracks this route starts from Chapel Stile to climb by Elterwater Quarry and through Baysbrown Wood crossing to ascend Lingmoor on its Little Langdale side. It then traverses the spine to gain Brown How - the summit of Lingmoor - before returning to descend the Great Langdale slopes directly to Chapel Stile.

THE ROUTE

Just below Wainwrights' Inn a little gate leads to a wooden footbridge crossing Great Langdale Beck. Bear right beyond the bridge and briefly follow the river to gain the track leading between the old stone abutments. Climb the track to gain the quarry road and bear right between the sheds of this working slate quarry. Bear left to leave the quarry and follow a track which gains a surfaced road by Crossgates House.

Opposite the house a path climbs steeply up the wooded hillside of Baysbrown Wood. Follow the path up through the wood before dropping down to gain the larger track of Ullet's

Nest which leads into Little Langdale. Go right to immediately pass through a gate and ascend the track. It levels and continues to make a final rise around a little knoll – the highest point of the track. After a further 100m a gate on the right leads out onto the fellside (before Dale End Farm).

Follow the path which winds its way up the Little Langdale flank of Lingmoor. As the shoulder is crested the path bears left. A little further along and down to the right there is a stile/gate leading through the stone wall – this will be taken in descent. Bear left from the main path ascending slightly to the

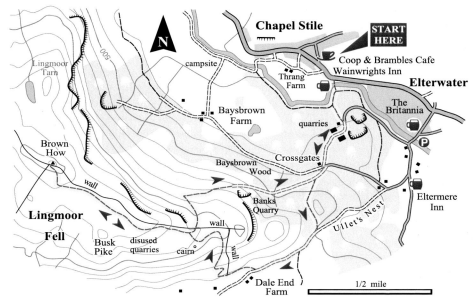

little Bield Crag Cairn – viewpoint looking out across Little Langdale to the Southern Fells with a particularly fine aspect over Little Langdale Tarn to Wetherlam and the Greenburn Horseshoe of fells.

Walking the spine of Lingmoor Fell - Langdale Pikes Beyond.

Cross to the centre of the shoulder to take the grassy track which rises steeply near the crest of the fell. A stone wall runs along to the right. Follow the path to skirt along the undulating spine of the fell. Beyond the final distinctive section of stone wall steep ascent climbs to the highest shoulder and a little way along this a stile leads right over the fence to the cairned summit knoll of Lingmoor – Brown How. Exalted position looking over the head of Little Langdale to the southern fells, over the head of Great Langdale to Pike O'Blisco, Crinkle Crags and Bowfell, over Lingmoor Tarn to the Langdale Pikes.

Make return by the same route to find the stile through the stone wall. Cross the stile, descending the grassy path to gain a track which leads right down to the abandoned slate level of Banks Quarry. Continue into Baysbrown Wood to intercept in a short way the path taken in ascent.

Brown How - the top of Lingmoor Fell

FACT SHEET
LENGTH: 7km
TIME: 3½ hours
DIFFICULTY: Difficult and rising to an altitude of 469m. Generally on good tracks though boggy in places with relatively strenuous ascent and descent
START & FINISH: Chapel Stile, limited parking within the perimeter of the village (323052)
ALTERNATIVE STARTS: Little Langdale Village, Elterwater Village, Elterwater Common
MAPS: OS L90 OR OL7
HOSTELRIES: Wainwrights' Inn and Brambles Café in Chapel Stile

WALK 8

THE GREAT LANGDALE VALLEY BOTTOM

Dominated by the high Langdale Pikes, Great Langdale, with its villages of Elterwater and Chapel Stile and its smattering of small farms dotted along its S shaped length, has long been one of the most celebrated mountain valleys in Great Britain. To savour the special atmosphere of this remarkable dale this walk makes an anticlockwise circuit around the valley bottom starting from the car parks beside The Stickle Barn and The New Dungeon Ghyll.

THE ROUTE

Take the road leading up the valley (west) for a short way until a gate on the left opens to the track which leads to Side House Farm. Pass through the farm and go left, following the boggy path up and across the open hillside. Descend slightly to intercept a narrow stone lane. Follow the lane along and then between stone walls to a barn by Oak Howe Farm (Oak How Needle stands on the fellside above).

Go right at the junction (away from the farm) and follow the track to enter woods a little way before Baysbrown Farm. Pass the farm, taking the surfaced road through the oaks and mixed deciduous Baysbrown Wood. Keep straight on, passing Crossgates House, following the surfaced road. Eventually this descends, after being intercepted by the stony track of Ullet's Nest falling from the right, to Elterwater. Turn left on the main road, The Elterwater Inn Bar lies just to the right. The village and The Britannia Inn lies just beyond the bridge over Great Langdale Beck. This route, however, bears left up the track/road which bears off immediately before the bridge.

Follow the road, used by quarry traffic, until steps lead down and right, to the banks of the river. Follow the path until the river is crossed by a wooden footbridge. Bear left along the road, Wainwrights' Inn to the left, until a point before and opposite Chapel Stile Village Hall and Public Toilets, a track rises off to the left.

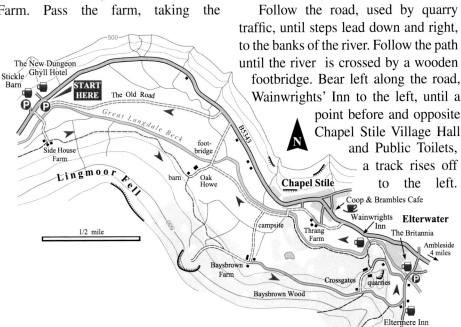

Follow the track and go left at the junction to pass the buildings by Thrang Farm to follow a short walled lane which leads to an open stony track. Go

Great Langdale Valley Bottom amongst the high fells

left along the track to cross New Bridge. Bear right following the track by the river bank and across the fields, through a number of gates, to find a wooden footbridge leading right over Great Langdale Beck. Cross this and ascend to a kissing gate opening to the main road. Go left for a short way until a stone lane leads off to the left – this is the Old Langdale Road and it leads, with

Signpost pointing up the track leaving Chapel Stile

great views to Langdale Pikes,Crinkle Cragsand Bowfell,directly back to the small car park opposite the entrance to The New Dungeon Ghyll Hotel.

Over Langdale Boulders to the Pikes

FACT SHEET
LENGTH: 10km
TIME: 3½ hours
DIFFICULTY: Easy
START & FINISH: Large car parks either side of the road near Stickle Barn and The New Dungeon Ghyll Hotel (295064)
ALTERNATIVE STARTS:
Elterwater, Chapel Stile, Baysbrown Campsite, Langdale Campsite.
MAPS: OS L90 OR OL7
HOSTELRIES ON ROUTE: Stickle Barn, New Dungeon Ghyll Hotel, Britannia Inn, Eltermere Inn, Wainwrights' Inn, Brambles Café

STICKLE TARN BY MILL GILL AND THE HORSE MEADOW

Fed by Bright Beck, Stickle Tarn occupies a little mountain basin below the great cliff of Pavey Ark. This route crosses behind Millbeck Farm to follow the 'outgang' onto the fell before a zigzag path climbs the west (true right) bank of Mill Gill to the walled horse meadow. The grass path above provides a splendid view over the tarn before descent from the dam takes the stone steps beneath Tarn Crag down to the regular Stickle Ghyll route.

THE ROUTE

Between the two Inns a gate leads to the main Stickle Ghyll path. Beyond the gate bear right to a footbridge over the beck. The slight path rises to cross the little beck by a large stone slab beneath a yew tree. A little gate leads to the walled lane, 'outgang', rising above the farm. Continue between the walls until above the lane the stream is crossed by a stone slab bridge. Climb the path for a little way until the going levels and a shoulder, with a boulder near the start, rises to the right. Go right to leave the main path and climb the narrow stony path up the shoulder which forms the west bank of Mill Gill. After a short ascent the narrow path zags to the left to traverse beneath a little crag and holly tree. The path zigs and zags before a path bears off ascending to the right. Don't continue traversing to the left. As the way slackens a constructed track leads right just above the head of Mill Gill before climbing left to the gap in the stone wall. The lower wall of the Horse Meadow - where the farm horses were brought each springtime. Rather boggy. Follow the path rising diagonally left through the 'meadow' to find a narrow stone gateway through the higher enclosing wall. Follow the grassy path rising up to the right.

At the highest point of this path, from where a climb to the left gives elevated views over Stickle Tarn, a little level shoulder is crossed. Beyond this slight descent leads to a well worn path. Go left and descend to Stickle Tarn. Bear left, stepping stones, taking the path beside the tarn to the dam. To visit the dam, a good place to take a break and admire the view, cross the tarn outflow balancing on the little rocks to keep the feet dry.

In descent keep left,

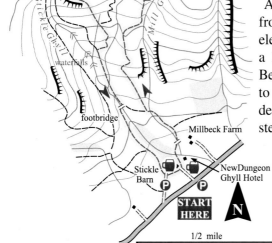

Over Stickle Tarn to the great precipice of Pavey Ark

following the path down the true left bank of Stickle Ghyll. After a short distance a rocky step lies in front. At this point a natural horizontal shelf leads off to the left avoiding the step. Traverse left along the path, moving away from the ghyll, to find a shoulder and little boulder marking the hidden head of an excellent path of stone steps. Follow the steps first traversing left beneath Tarn Crag and then making more direct descent down to intercept the main path by the true left bank of Stickle Ghyll.

Millbeck Farm with Stickle Ghyll behind

Descend the main path, by a series of stone steps, until it levels. Cross the little stream near the ruined stone sheep folds, following the path, until in a little way a stile leads off down to the right descending the true left bank of Stickle Ghyll until a footbridge is crossed. Continue down the path above the ghyll to the starting point.

FACT SHEET
LENGTH: 3½km
TIME: 2½ hours
DIFFICULTY: Difficult with strenuous ascent (400m) and steep descent
START & FINISH: Large car parks either side of the road near Stickle Barn and the New Dungeon Ghyll Hotel (295064).
ALTERNATIVE STARTS: None
MAPS: OS L90 OR OL6
NEAREST WATERING HOLES: Stickle Barn and New Dungeon Ghyll Hotel

WALK 10

BETWEEN THE DUNGEON GHYLLS

At the driveable head of Great Langdale there are two famous Hotels, separated by the Stickle Barn Inn, the Old and the New Dungeon Ghyll. Long popular with mountaineers they are named after the dramatic and deeply cut natural rift of the Dungeon Ghyll which, complete with fine waterfalls, falls from the heights of The Langdale Pikes. Utilising a high ancient packhorse route, and the path across the low meadows, this walk circumnavigates between the two, twice crossing the stream flowing from the Dungeon Ghyll.

FACT SHEET
LENGTH: 2½km
TIME: 1 hour
DIFFICULTY: Easy
START & FINISH: Stickle Ghyll Nat Trust car park (295064)
ALTERNATIVE STARTS: Car park on opposite side of road or Old Dungeon Ghyll
MAPS: OS L90 or OL6
HOSTELRIES: The Stickle Barn, New Dungeon Ghyll Hotel, Old Dungeon Ghyll Hotel

At the end of the day

THE ROUTE

From the head of the car park follow the path around the back of the Stickle Barn and out onto the main path. Go left through the gap and immediately turn left to ascend a rough stony track to a kissing gate at the top of the rise. Continue straight on the track falling to cross the footbridge over Dungeon Ghyll. Keep along the walled lane until at a point above the Old Dungeon Ghyll

Hotel, a kissing gate leads to an open area. Descend and cross the stream to find a little gate on the opposite side of the track below. Pass through the gate and descend by the wall, with the Old Dungeon Ghyll to the left and Middlefell Farm to the right. A little gate leads to the road junction. Over the road, to the left, a gate leads into the flat meadow.

Walk across the meadow parallel to Great Langdale Beck until the path, beneath the distinct mound of Kirk Howe, pulls away to the left to find a wooden sleeper foot-bridge crossing the lower

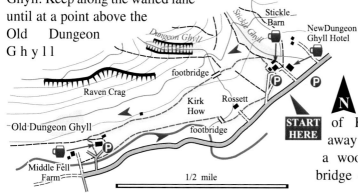

The rift of the Dungeon Ghyll falls centrally between The Pikes; gateway to the fells the Old Hotel stands to the left, Stickle Barn and the New Hotel to the right

section of the Dungeon Ghyll. Go right across the bridge then immediately left. Walk on to pass the farmstead of Rossett, sheltered in the trees to the left. The gate ahead leads directly into the car park.

The low path across the meadows from Stickle Ghyll car park

WALK 11

LANGDALE PIKES BY STICKLE TARN

A justifiably popular and scenic route to ascend the two major tops of The Langdale Pikes; Harrison Stickle and Pike O'Stickle. Stickle Ghyll is ascended to Stickle Tarn Dam followed by the main path to the top of Harrison Stickle. A short descent and traverse leads to the scrambly top of Pike O'Stickle before a good path descends beneath Thorn Crag and on down the shoulder of Mark Gate.

THE ROUTE

Leave the head of the Stickle Barn Car Park by the little path and continue to turn left and follow up the main trod beside the stream of Stickle Ghyll. A footbridge leads right over the ghyll to its true left bank. Follow the path, over a stile, and continue to make ascent of the stone paved route. Above the waterfalls the going slackens for a while until a craggy outcrop stands to the right and the path rounds a corner. Beneath a scrambly rock step it is easier to go left across the ghyll by the purposely placed stone slabs to gain its true right bank.

Continue to make scrambly ascent to reach the end of the stone embankment of Stickle Dam.

A path traverses left above the shore of the lake, rising to make steep ascent to the right of the nose of Harrison Stickle. Intercept a horizontal path and go left following the path around to make ascent directly to the summit of Harrison Stickle. Head north from the summit rocks to the grassy shoulder beyond, from where a path falls leftwards into a hollow. Cross the peat bog by the paving stones and follow the path rightwards to the distinct rocky cone of Pike O'Stickle. Scrambly paths rise to the left and the right and gain the summit cairn. Make descent by the same route and follow the approach path for only a little way until another well worn

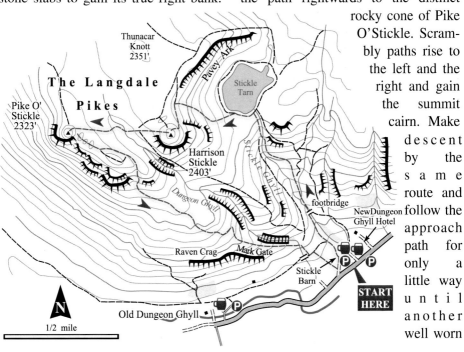

path ascends off to the right.

Take the easiest route, which mostly avoids the crest of the ridge and the top of Loft Crag, until the broad top of a gully is reached. The terraced tops to the left are those of Thorn Crag. Follow the path down right until the way slackens. Traverse the grassy shoulder then,

The Langdale Pikes

just beyond a cairn, bear right to find the pathway which leads left across the terraces before zigzagging down to gain the long shoulder of Mark Gate. The rift of Dungeon Ghyll lies down to the left. Near the bottom encounter a stone wall and descend by it to gain the stream of Dungeon Ghyll. Cross the ghyll to find a stile and go right over this. Descend the path by the wall until a track is intercepted. Go left through the gate until in a little way a kissing gate on the right

leads to a path descending to the body of the large car park by Stickle Barn.

Harrison Stickle left, from Pike O'Stickle

Crossing Stickle Ghyll

Over Stickle Tarn Dam to Harrison Stickle

FACT SHEET
LENGTH: 5½km
TIME: 4 hours
DIFFICULTY: Very difficult mountain route with strenuous ascent (some 700m) and descent. The ascent of Pike O'Stickle constitutes a mild scramble requiring use of hands as well as feet.
START & FINISH: Large car parks either side of the road near Stickle Barn and The New Dungeon Ghyll Hotel (295064)
ALTERNATIVE STARTS: The Old Dungeon Ghyll lies 1km to the west.
MAPS: OS L90 or OL6
HOSTELRIES: Stickle Barn and New Dungeon Ghyll Hotel

WALK 12

TO BOWFELL

Bowfell is the highest of the mountains above The Langdales - a much prized summit. This circular walk passes through Stool End Farm and climbs The Band to Three Tarns col before ascending the final rocky shoulder to the summit knoll. After continuation across the shoulder descent is made to Ore Gap and down to the Esk Hause track by Angle Tarn. Rossett Gill zigzags lead down to Mickleden and a flat track returns to the start.

FACT SHEET
LENGTH: 13km
TIME: 6 hours
DIFFICULTY: Very difficult, a long, high mountain route with strenuous ascent (some 900m) and descent
START & FINISH: Nat Trust car park at The Old Dungeon Ghyll (286061)
ALTERNATIVE STARTS: The Stickle Barn lies 1km to the west
MAPS: OS L90 OR OL6
HOSTELRIES: Old Dungeon Ghyll Hotel

Seen above Three Tarns col the high shoulder of Bowfell with it's pyramidal summit cone to the left

THE ROUTE

Gain the road and go right until, where the road does a 90 degrees left, a gate leads straight on up a long drive up to Stool End Farm. Go through the farm taking the path rising to the left. After a short way a path rises to the right and continues beyond a gate to make steep ascent up the nose of the long shoulder known as The Band. Follow the good path all the way up to the col of Three Tarns. Ascend to the right following the stony path onto the

The lane to Stool End Farm with The Band above and Bowfell right

shoulder and traverse along this until the path climbs back left up to the rocky summit knoll of Bowfell.

Descend and head north along the shoulder bearing down left to make descent into the col known as Ore Gap. Descend from the col following the stony path down to the right (north). The path leads down across the fellside to intercept the Esk Hause path a little above Angle Tarn. Descend to the right to pass the bottom of the tarn and make ascent to the top of Rossett Gill. After a short descent traverse right, away from the head of the gill, to gain and make descent by the stone pathway known as the Rossett Gill Zigzags. As the going

levels at the head of Mickleden pass a stone sheepfold (Stake Pass climbs to Borrowdale at this point) and cross a wooden footbridge. Follow the fairly level footpath along the valley bottom and on between the stone walls all the way back to The Old Dungeon Ghyll Hotel.

A perfect mountain sanctuary - the middle tarn of Three Tarns with The Scafells seen beyond. The final shoulder of Bowfell rises to the right from this point

WALK 13

TO PIKE O'BLISCO

There is something rascallian about Blisco - it cocks a snoop at all its impressive neighbours and makes a wonderful walk. A circular outing starting from The Old Dungeon Ghyll to rise from Blea Tarn Pass by Redacre Gill to the summit of Pike O'Blisco. Descent to Red Tarn leads to the Browney Gill footpath falling into Oxendale. Return is made through Stool End Farm and along the valley bottom.

THE ROUTE

Gain the road and follow it up the valley. Cross the cattle grid by a barn, belonging to Wall End Farm, at the foot of Blea Tarn Pass. Ascend until at the top of the zigzags a track leads off to the right. Take this and continue along the path to cross the streams and make steep ascent above Redacre Gill. The path levels and bears right before climbing through terraces to gain the col between the two rocky knolls which constitute the top of Pike O'Blisco. The cairned top to the right is the summit.

Return to the col and bear right (south west) to make stony descent to intercept the horizontal path just beyond the bottom of Red Tarn. Bear right and go right again at the junction to make descent down the true right bank of Browney Gill. The path descends into Oxendale and crosses a wooden footbridge. Go right through the stone sheepfold and make slight ascent before the path drops to Stool End Farm. Go through the farm and continue along the track back to the Nat Trust car park at The Old Dungeon Ghyll.

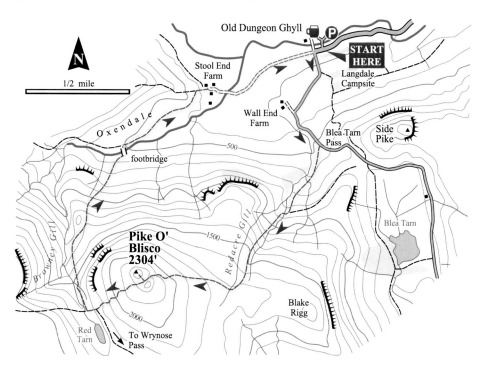

The cone of Pike O'Blisco with, to its right, Browney Gill falling from Red Tarn into Oxendale

Descending to Oxendale with The Pikes beyond

"Get down Will" - summit cairn Pike O'Blisco

FACT SHEET
LENGTH: 8km
TIME: 4 hours
DIFFICULTY: A mildly difficult mountain route with strenuous ascent (some 700m) and descent
START & FINISH: Nat Trust car park at The Old Dungeon Ghyll (286061)
ALTERNATIVE STARTS: The Stickle Barn lies 1km to the west, limited parking near the foot of Blea Tarn Pass
MAPS: OS L90 or OL6
HOSTELRIES: Old Dungeon Ghyll Hotel

A CIRCUIT OF BLEA TARN
(PLUS ALTERNATIVE – A CLIMB TO SIDE PIKE)

The sublime Blea Tarn nests in splendid isolation suspended between the two Langdales, Little and Great. This walk makes a simple clockwise perambulation of the tarn walking through the plantation to the little Scots Pine clad headland on the west shore before continuing to the head of the pass. Return is made via the road passing Blea Tarn House and the Echo Stone. For the energetic the extra ascent of Side Pike is also described.

THE ROUTE

An iconic Lakeland beauty - little Blea Tarn has many moods and this is a walk for all seasons. Take the gate on the opposite side of the road to the car park and follow the level pathway to enter the trees. Cross the little wooden footbridge over the stream which issue from the tarn. Go right. At a point where the path bears left away from the edge of the tarn walk right to the rocky viewpoint and its stand of Scots Pine. Return to the main path and follow it to leave the woods. Continue along the pathway which rises slowly contouring easily to the cattle grid at the head of the Blea Tarn Pass.

The alternative route climbing Side Pike takes the stile on the opposite side of the road before first bearing left then ascending back right to climb the shoulder of the pike on a well worn path. Pass over the shoulder and a rock knoll and drop to a little level col. Continue to the rocky summit point with staggering views across the head of Great Langdale to the Langdale Pikes, Bowfell and Crinkle Crags. Take care for steep cliffs lie directly below the summit cone – no safe passage straight on. Descend taking the route of ascent to the col to find a lesser path breaking down to the left. Slight descent leads to a contour left beneath the rocky Blea Tarn face of the pike to a narrow rock squeeze between a large rock flake and the crag – 'Fat Man's Agony'. Pass through this, difficulty dependent on girth, to follow the path descending to a little stile over the wire fence. Steep grassy descent leads to the road.

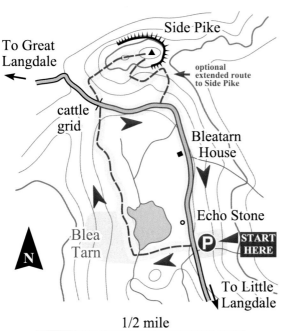

Side Pike

To Great Langdale

optional extended route to Side Pike

cattle grid

Bleatarn House

Echo Stone

Blea Tarn

START HERE

N

To Little Langdale

1/2 mile

Ice on Blea Tarn - Side Pike to the right, Langdale Pikes seen centrally

The regular route avoiding the ascent of Side Pike bears right to follow the narrow undulating road. Beware of traffic around the blind bends. Pass beneath the bent larch by Bleatarn House, ascend the steep hill beyond, to continue more easily above the tarn. Note the boulder, right side of the road, just before the car park – the Echo Stone. A shout over the tarn, in ideal conditions, can produce seven echoes. Go on!

FACT SHEET
LENGTH: 2½km (3km with alt)
TIME: 1½ hours (2½ hours with alt)
DIFFICULTY: Very easy (Difficult with Altnerative addition)
START & FINISH: Blea Tarn car park (296043)
ALTERNATIVE STARTS: Head of Blea Tarn Pass
MAPS: OS L90 OR OL7
HOSTELRIES: Nearest - Old Dungeon Ghyll Hotel in Great Langdale, Three Shires Inn in Little Langdale

Fat Man's Agony - Side Pike

On The Echo Stone

WALK 15

TWO TARNS LITTLE LANGDALE

A fine anticlockwise exploration of the head of Little Langdale, passing Blea Tarn before falling to round Little Langdale Tarn and make high return along Lingmoor's fell wall. Castle Howe, Fell Foot's Viking Ting Mound, Hall Garth, Slaters Bridge, High Birk Howe Farm, Dale End Farm, The Bield and The Busk offer features of some 7,000 years of man's involvement with the landcape. Stunning natural scenery, beneath high fells, throughout.

THE ROUTE

Take the gate opposite the car park and follow the track, passing Blea Tarn, on and down to a little footbridge. Cross the bridge and go left taking the path down to Blea Moss. Bear right taking the high route above the moss and WW1 targets to intercept the Roman road of Wrynose Pass. Go left and descend with the road to pass defensive site Castle Howe and down to the right angled bend at the bottom of the hill. Just above on the right a gate gives access to the Viking Ting Mound. Walk past Fell Foot Farm and its 17th C smugglers porch following the road to the old stone arched Fell Foot Bridge and go right along the

FACT SHEET
LENGTH: 8½km
TIME: 3 hours
DIFFICULTY: Easy though making descent and ascent (some 700m combined)
START & FINISH: National Trust car park at Blea Tarn (300044)
ALTERNATIVE START: Limited parking in the centre of Little Langdale
MAPS: OS L90 or OL6 + OL7
HOSTELRIES: Nearest are Three Shires Inn and Old Dungeon Ghyll Hotel

lane. Go over the bridge to pass Bridge End Farm to rise with the track. At the junctions keep left along the track to cross a little stream, pass through a gate and descend past the 15th C farmsteads of High and Low Hallgarth. A little further along the lane a kissing gate/stile lead down to the ancient Slaters Bridge.

Cross the bridge and climb steeply, up past the whaleback rock, to

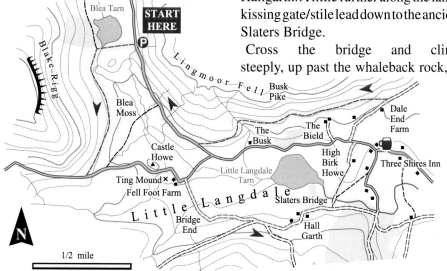

Over Little Langdale Tarn from the High Birk Howe Lane

follow the path to Birk Howe Farm lane. Go left to the road. Left then right following the little road to Dale End Farm. Pass the farm and continue along the track through a gate and on a little way until a kissing gate to the left leads to a path climbing up Lingmoor Fell. Go through two little gates until above the second gate a path traverses off left to follow above the fell wall. Traverse the path, above the buildings of The Bield and The Busk, continuing until the way opens between walls above and below (outgang), keep high to drop on a little track to the road. Go right and follow it, above Blea Moss Common and Bronze Age 'stone circle', to climb the final steep hill to cross the cattle grid and back to the car park.

Bridge End Farm

Blea Tarn

WALK 16

CRINKLE CRAGS FROM THE THREE SHIRES STONE

The Crinkle Crags form the rugged, serrated skyline above Oxendale at the head of Great Langdale. This walk approaches from the Three Shires Stone at the head of Wrynose Pass. Traverse by Red Tarn, to ascend the broad shoulder of Great Knott and gain The Crinkles which are traversed to Three Tarns col before making return over much the same route. (Alternatively if suitable transport arrangements are made descent can be made down The Band from Three Tarns.)

THE ROUTE

Parking is limited around the head of Wrynose Pass. Circumnavigate the bog and follow the well defined path making reasonably gentle ascent until the going levels and Red Tarn can be seen down to the left. Beyond the tarn, at the junction of paths, bear left and follow the unmistakeable stony path up the broad shoulder of Great Knott to the rocky knoll of the First Crinkle. Descend into the gap beyond. Straight ahead is a scramble grade 2 - The Bad Step. The walking route avoids this by traversing left to climb a

FACT SHEET
LENGTH: 12km
TIME: 6 hours
DIFFICULTY: A difficult and long mountain route with strenuous ascent (some 800m) and descent, sections of scrambling can be avoided.
START & FINISH: Head of Wrynose Pass (277028)
ALTERNATIVE FINISH: Descent can be made down The Band from Three Tarns.
MAPS: OS L90 or OL6
HOSTELRIES: Nearest are Old Dungeon Ghyll Hotel and Three Shires Inn

broad gully, rising to gain the highest cairn, balanced on a rock edge, the top of Long Top.

Follow the path down right and cross the gap of Mickle Dore to make slight ascent and then descent, with a little tarn down below to the left, following the main path on the west side of the rock knolls. From a gap climb Shelter Crags taking the path over its shoulder to find a little tarn in a hollow. Continue with slight ascent then rough stone descent leading to Three Tarns col. The highest of these tarns is now miniscule. Return to the Three

Bowfell 2960'
Bowfell Links
Buskoe Sike
Three Tarns
Shelter Crags
Crinkle Crags
Long Top
Bad Step
Pike O' Blisco
Red Tarn
Black Crag
Cold Pike
Little Stand
To Little Langdale
Three Shires Stone
START HERE
Wrynose Pass
N
1/2 mile

Crinkle Crags above the Oxendale head of Great Langdale

Long Top from 1st Crinkle

easier to avoid ascent of the First Crinkle by taking the grassy path traversing below the crest to the right.

Three Shires Stone

Shires Stone by the same route or alternatively descend The Band to Stool End Farm if suitable transport arrangements have been made. If returning by The Crinkles then it is recommended that the walking descent is followed bearing right from the summit cairn of Long Top to find a cairn at the head of the broad gully (on the Eskdale side). In the gap beyond it is

To Mickle Dore from Long Top

WETHERLAM AND THE GREENBURN HORSESHOE

Located on the southern margins of The Langdales this is a glorious round, long and strenuous, with breathtaking scenery. Begin in Little Langdale and cross the Ford Bridge to find the Greenburn track and a climb onto Birks Fell. The Wetherlam Edge leads to Wetherlam before a drop and slog up the Prison Band opens up the rest of the horseshoe - Swirl How and Carrs. Descent of Wet Side Edge falls to a footbridge afterwhich the Greenburn track is regained.

THE ROUTE

Follow the road down to cross the Ford Bridge. Turn right and keep along the track to rise past Hall Garth cottages. Continue through the gate and up the stony track passing the first junction until, at point where the track begins to descend, a track bears off rising to the left. Follow the track until, in 600 metres, a little footpath rises diagonally left up the fellside. Cross the ladder stile and climb the shoulder until the path bears off to the right. Cross a stile over the fence and climb until a further stile crosses to the right. Rise with the path taking the zigzag path up the open nose of Birk Fell. Cross Birk Fell to gain the rocky path

rising up the nose of Wetherlam. The easiest route, a little scrambly in places, keeps to the right and climbs to gain the summit cairn of Wetherlam.

A good path descends and traverses the shoulder to the west before dropping into the col of Swirl Hawse. Climb the steep rocky rib of Prison Band directly to the cairned top of Swirl How. The main path traverses the rim down to Broad Slack (up and left can be found the remains of crashed Halifax Bomber 'S for Sugar') and then climbs again to the top of Great Carrs. The path is well worn and descends steeply over a rocky knoll, left

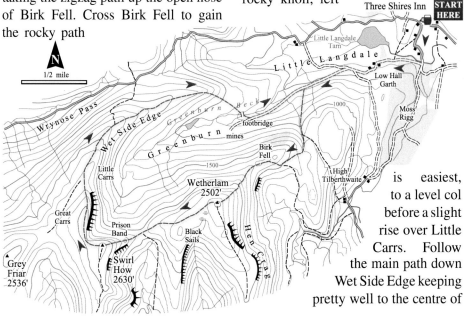

is easiest, to a level col before a slight rise over Little Carrs. Follow the main path down Wet Side Edge keeping pretty well to the centre of

Wetherlam and The Greenburn Horseshoe above Little Langdale Tarn

the shoulder. Do not descend to the left.

Nearing the end of the shoulder, beyond High End, a path drops down to the right. Descend steeply at first until the going eases and becomes a little boggy in places. Bear right to follow down the right side of a stone wall which falls to Greenburn Beck and a footbridge located below the ruined mine buildings. Cross the bridge and ascend to the Greenburn track, go left and retrace the route back to the start.

Memorial to crashed Halifax 'S for Sugar'

FACT SHEET
LENGTH: 14km
TIME: 6 hours
DIFFICULTY: A very difficult and long mountain route with strenuous ascent (some 1000m) and descent, rough and scrambly in places
START & FINISH: Limited parking in the centre of Little Langdale (316034)
ALTERNATIVE START: No parking
MAPS: OS L90 or OL6 + OL7
HOSTELRIES: Three Shires Inn

WALK 18

SLATERS BRIDGE, THE CATHEDRAL AND HIGH TILBERTHWAITE

Mixed woods, the much loved Slaters Bridge, the amazing Cathedral Quarry and open aspect and great views across the High Tilberthwaite Pass make this a very fulfilling walk. You don't have to take the alternative through the quarry tunnels; the walk is glorious with or without this section. Indeed the tunnels are scrambly, dark, wet and full of potential danger - children love them - but have a care.

THE ROUTE

Follow the road down towards the Ford until, past Low Birk Howe House, steps and kissing gate on the right lead to a little path. Follow the path over the low shoulder and drop to Slaters Bridge – a special place. Cross the bridge and up to a stile and kissing gate leading onto a stony lane. Turn left, go on through a gate and rise until a gate and stile on the right lead up onto the slate quarry bank. Bear right through the short tunnel into the spectacular Cathedral Quarry. Return to the quarry bank outside and go back down to the lane and turn right. Continue along the track to pass the Ford and rise right to a junction. (Alternatively, for the adventurous with a torch and wellies, it is possible to follow a route through the mountain; gain the open hole beyond the large chamber and scramble up until beneath the undercut sheer wall. Below is a tunnel which is followed, taking left fork, to emerge onto a bank above the regular track. Descend and go right).

Bear right and keep along the track, with the lovely mixed oak woods of Moss Rigg up to the right, to a junction (1km). Bear right and continue until, down a little hill, the farm of High Tilberthwaite lies in front (1km). Go through the gate into the farmyard and immediately turn right through a gate to rise up a stone track. (Alternatively go right on a little path before the farm to make a shortcut between the tracks). Stay on the track, High Tilberthwaite Pass, and over the summit down to Little Langdale. At the junction of tracks go right. Cross the little stream, gate, go down past the

Three Shires Inn

START HERE

Little Langdale Tarn

Slaters Bridge

Little Langdale

Low Hall Garth

ford

Cathedral Quarry

alternative route through tunnels

Moss Rigg Wood

-1000-

High Tilberthwaite Pass

Betsy Crag

High Tilberthwaite Farm

N

1/2 mile

Slaters Bridge; stone arch and Devil's Slab

High and Low Hall Garth, and on to the kissing gate and stile above Slaters Bridge. Return via the route taken in approach.

Track to Tilberthwaite by Moss Rigg Woods

Cathedral Quarry; pool and pillar

FACT SHEET
LENGTH: 6km
TIME: 2 hours
DIFFICULTY: Easy walking with a little ascent (some 265m) and descent. If the tunnel option is taken it's a little scrambly and adds a further dimension
START & FINISH: Limited Parking centre of Little Langdale (316034)
ALTERNATIVE START: Tilberthwaite
MAPS: OS L90 or OL7
HOSTELRIES: Three Shires Inn

HODGE CLOSE AND HOLME FELL FROM LITTLE LANGDALE

Seen from the centre of Little Langdale village, whimsically punctuated with trees along
its crest, Holme Fell forms the knobbly southern skyline. This walk takes you on a
journey deep through the oakwoods and up out onto the crest to reveal a panoramic view
that covers the full range of Central Fells – including Helvellyn and Fairfield, plus
Lingmoor and the High Langdale Fells beyond, and the king and queen of the Southern
Fells - Coniston Old Man and Wetherlam. Look out over Yew Tree Tarn, Coniston Water
and the Holme Fell Tarns before descent leads past the huge gaping hole of Hodge Close
Quarry to return once again into the woods.

THE ROUTE

Take the road down to the Ford. Once
across the bridge, bear left. At the junction keep left and follow the track/road
to the buildings of Stang End. Turn right
immediately
after the barn
and continue
along the track
through various
gates
to

reach the edge of the hamlet of Hodge
Close. Bear left, above the garage,
to join a further track. Left again and
follow this track along to pass
through High Oxenfell Farm.
Continue up the road, go straight on at the
junction. Crest the hill to find, just
beyond, above the road on the right, a
wooden gate. Pass through the gate and
follow the narrow path rising to the right,
through the bracken, over the shoulder.
There are a number of paths along the
shoulder. The easiest tend to be just off
the crest whilst the best viewpoints are
obviously on top of the many bumps.

Traverse along the path then move
diagonally left to rise into a little
corridor between the tops. Beyond, a
little climb leads to a stile and a heath-
ery top. View over Yew Tree Tarn and
Coniston Water. Go right descending
by the old iron fence to a dip. Climb up
and left traversing below the 1st knoll
and cross a little valley. Climb up to
the shoulder just right of the large 2nd
knoll to a silver birch to find the path
traverses easily left on the northern
side of the knoll. Cross to another
valley and contour left past the knoll
to gain yet another valley. Climb the
knoll behind and traverse left along

Three
Shires
Inn
START
HERE

Little
Langdale

Slaters
Bridge

ford and
footbridge

Stang End

Little
Fell

Moss
Rigg
Wood

Hodge
Close

High
Oxenfell
Farm

gate

Hodge
Close
Quarry

Holme
Ground

Holme
Fell
Tarns

Uskdale Gap

N

Holme Fell
995'

1/2 mile

Yew
Tree
Tarn

High
Yewdale   A593

FACT SHEET
LENGTH: 9km
TIME: 3-4 hours
DIFFICULTY: Mildly difficult with ascent
(some 450m) and descent
START & FINISH: Limited Parking centre
of Little Langdale (316034)
ALTERNATIVE START: Parking at Hodge
Close Quarry
MAPS: OS L90 or OL7
HOSTELRIES: Three Shires Inn

Holme Fell Tarn

its shoulder to fall again into a further valley. Climb up the left side of the final bump to a col on its shoulder. Below lies the valley crossing of Uskdale Gap and ahead the real, anvil shaped, tops of Holme Fell. The first top sports a large cairn, from this point traverse easily across the high shoulder to the next long shoulder - beyond yet another distinct valley. A little climb leads to the summit knoll of Holme Fell, actually an elongated ridge which runs from the Little Langdale to the Coniston side. A cairned rock in the middle is taken as the nominal top, though the rocky knolls either side may be higher.

Walk to the north and descend the path, various routes, toward the little Holme Fell Tarn, a dammed reservoir. Pass the tarn, take either side, to find at its foot a path leading down to the right. Descend this, passing a quarry bank, down to intercept a track. Turn right and continue to the great hole of Hodge Close Quarry. Pass the quarry by it's left side and take the road down into the hamlet of Hodge Close. Bear left and follow the track on down to a stone slab foot-bridge at the   bottom of the valley. Rise up the track b e y o n d and turn right at the junc-t i o n . This is the track l e a d i n g by Moss R i g g W o o d back to the Ford.

Holme Fell over Little Langdale

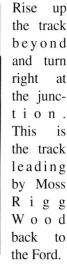

WALK 20

COLWITH FORCE VIA LOW HACKET AND STANG END

This interesting scenic route makes a clockwise perambulation around the Little Langdale valley. Descending on the north side and rising on the south it is an outing suitable for all seasons and most conditions. From the centre of the village pass the Three Shires Inn, Wilson Place Farm and Low Hacket to cross the River Brathay by Colwith Bridge before rising by Colwith Force Waterfall, High Park and Stang End to re-cross the river by Lang Parrock Footbridge.

THE ROUTE

Take the road down through the village past the Three Shires Inn until, by a cottage on the left, a lane rises to Wilson Place Farm. Just before the farmhouse a track branches to the right (with a cottage to its right). Go through the gate and follow up the field until at its top a path bears off to the left. Go through the little gate and bear right up a few steps and through a little iron gate. Traverse the field with a little oakwood to the left. A gap in the wall leads to another field. A little stand of trees shields the house of Low Hacket. Bear right across to the corner and a stone stile then bear left to find another

FACT SHEET
LENGTH: *4½km*
TIME: *1-1½ hours*
DIFFICULTY: *Easy though making descent and ascent (some 400m combined) for much of it's length*
START & FINISH: *Limited Parking centre of Little Langdale (316034)*
ALTERNATIVE START: *Very limited parking south of Colwith Bridge*
MAPS: *OS L90 or OL7*
HOSTELRIES: *Three Shires Inn*

stone stile. The house of High Hacket is now above behind the trees. Cross the stile and continue to another stone stile which gives access to the driveway to the house (the public footpath). Go right down the drive and out through a

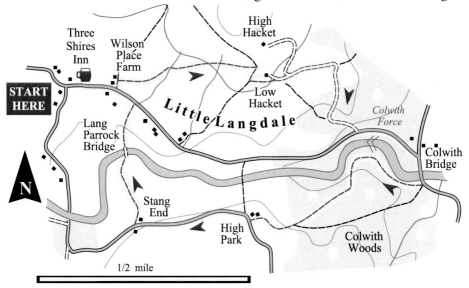

Looking over Wilson Place Farm and the village of Little Langdale

gate. Follow the track right, in front of the barn, and continue to descend the wide track all the way to the road. Bear left down the road. At the junction turn right and cross Colwith bridge.

Immediately on the right a stile leads to a little footpath traversing above the river to a rock viewpoint looking to the magnificent Colwith Force. Retrace steps slightly to climb stone steps and follow the path above the river (exposed drop – care) until the path begins to pull away, rising through the woods to the left. Exit into the meadow and follow the path to the buildings of High Park Farm. Go right and left through the buildings to exit onto a surfaced road. Bear right and continue to the white buildings of Stang End. Drop right past the end house, turn right through a gate beneath the houses. Through another

gate, a lane and meadow descend to Lang Parrock Footbridge. Cross and continue up the field to the road. Turn left and return to start.

Colwith Force waterfall

Visit Wainwrights' Inn and enjoy the warm and friendly atmosphere. Located in the heart of the breathtaking Langdale Valley, the Inn is a favourite with walkers and campers alike.

Choose from a variety of fine local ales, fine wines and an excellent menu created from the finest, locally sourced, fresh seasonal ingredients.

Wainwrights' Inn
Chapel Stile
Nr Ambleside
LA22 9JD

015394 38088
wainwrightsinn@langdale.co.uk
www.langdale.co.uk